JIM & DAVE DEFEAT
THE MASKED MAN

Cover design by Charles Orr.
Interior design by Shanna Compton.
All illustrations © Archie Rand.

Soft Skull Press
55 Washington Street
Suite 804
Brooklyn, NY 11201
www.softskull.com

Distributed by Publishers Group West.
1-800-788-3123 | www.pgw.com
Printed in Canada

Library of Congress Cataloging-in-Publication Data is avilable for this title.

Jim and Dave Defeat the Masked Man

JIM & DAVE DEFEAT THE MASKED MAN

Sestinas by
James Cummins & David Lehman
Illustrated by Archie Rand

With guest appearances by
Beth Ann Fennelly
& William Wadsworth

Foreword by Denise Duhamel

.

Foreword

Foreword

James Cummins and David Lehman have written a book, *Jim & Dave Defeat the Masked Man,* in which identity is intentionally blurred, disguised, and traded. Which poet has written which poem? Which poet is Superman and which is Clark Kent? Who is Batman and who Bruce Wayne? Who is Spiderman and who Peter Parker? Which poet is Zorro and which is Don Diego? There's a table of contents, to be sure, but it's in the form of a sestina written by one of the chaps and it proceeds by clues and hints rather than ready identifications. You have to wait until the end of the book before you arrive at a conventional list indicating which gentleman is responsible for which sestina.

Though one may wonder, "Who is the masked man that James Cummins and David Lehman defeat?" a more interesting question is, "Who are the masked men writing these poems? And what has drawn them to the sestina as the perfect form for their creative antics?" As the two sestina-meisters take turns writing individual poems (and collaborating on one together), the mild-mannered bespectacled lad and the dashing superhero that coexist inside both Cummins and Lehman rescue the form from the clutches of everyday life and transform it into something fantastic.

Maybe Cummins and Lehman are the literary grandsons of Tristan Tzara, who challenged private ownership and even the private and coherent lyrical self. They almost certainly owe a filial debt to John Ashbery and Kenneth Koch, whose collaborative sestina "Crone Rhapsody" (c. 1956) set a precedent for the adventures of Jim and Dave. But when Cummins and Lehman collaborate, they create something altogether new and attractively unusual. The act of collaborating has given them permission to go beyond their individual poetic practices, and we are the richer for it.

Going beyond the intrusion of the "authorial I" Cummins and Lehman make themselves characters in their own narratives. The authors double as actors who take over the script they're in. Each can impersonate the other in his absence, and both get to improvise. Their passion and verve synergize further than their separate intentions; their joint endeavor encourages an interaction between their public and private selves, a way around inhibition and reserve. The authors even conjure up a character named Denise Duhamel and rescue her from an insufferable writers' conference, presumably so that she can return home to write this foreword.

And as Denise learns—I mean as I do—these boys will be boys will be bosses! Cummins and Lehman use the six ending words characteristic of sestinas as a sixth sense into the politics of war, romance, and the games that the literati play. Marvin Bell, Anne Sexton, Walt Whitman, Ted Berrigan, Phillip Levine, Gary Snyder, and Rimbaud are all honorary end words. Bob Hass, Grace Paley, Rilke, Breton, Eluard, Reverdy, "Jorie" and "Kenneth" make appearances in these poems. Marvin Bell is transformed to Marvin Gardens in "Monopolies: A Sentimental Education." And Cummins and Lehman do indeed educate—slyly, with a wink and a nod, with telltale chalk dusting their superhero capes. But more importantly, their conspiracies and constraints engage their muse, a Catwoman who, in this book, is on the right side of the law. She helps the poets to subvert, with sublime effects, the poetic conventions they invoke. She gets them to tap into something bigger and more interesting than logic or reason.

The spirit of collaboration is infectious, and this book has grown accordingly. Guest poet Beth Ann Fennelly, responding to a line in Lehman's "masked man" sestina, wrote a high-spirited letter to the authors, and Cummins translated part of it into a pair of six-line stanzas. Challenged by Cummins to turn the sample stanzas into a complete sestina, Fennelly wrote "To James Cummins & David Lehman on the Opening of the Sestina Bar," and the fellows promptly made room for it in the book. Guest poet William Wadsworth collaborated with Lehman on the "Falstaff" sestina, which they wrote for the "lies" issue of *Tin House* magazine. They knew an essay on the Ern Malley poetry hoax was scheduled to run in that issue, so they published "Falstaff" under the name Jill Malley Reynolds, a granddaughter of the late Ethel Malley, the fictive Ern's older sister. Authorial identity is seldom so blissfully fluid.[1]

In his "Preface" to *The Nigger of the Narcissus,* Joseph Conrad writes, "The artist appeals to that part of our being which is not dependent on wisdom; to that in us which is a gift and not an acquisition—and, therefore, more permanently enduring." Cummins and Lehman give this gift to each other and to us. Sitting behind their desks or standing in the shadows, the two of them are ready to spring into action and save poetry just when it needs it most.

Denise Duhamel
Hollywood, FL
December 2004

---

1. According to the contributor's note in *Tin House,* Jill Malley Reynolds grew up in Melbourne, Australia, and was educated at the university at Perth and later at Cambridge University in England. She has lived north of Boston since 1994 and has written a monograph about John Ashbery's influence on Australian poets John Forbes and John Tranter: *Dear John* (Monograph Press, 2000). She has poems forthcoming in the online journal *Disquieting Muses.* The late Ethel Malley was her grandmother.

Preface

Preface

It is the honorable characteristic of Poetry that its materials are to be found in every subject which can interest the human mind. The evidence of this fact is to be sought, not in the writings of Critics, but in those of Poets themselves.

The majority of the following poems are to be considered as experiments. They were written chiefly with a view to ascertain the ratio of pressure to success in the execution of a maneuver be it in the competing realms of athletics or aesthetics, and whether two practitioners living in different places can, under conditions that scarcely resemble one another, and without the advantage of frequent meetings, produce the several poems that are collected in this volume and that manifest the authors' affection for an exotic formal device of rare Italian origin, artificial in the extreme and in no wise committed to the delineation of proper passions and plausible incidents but on the contrary delighting in all that mingles the natural and supernatural worlds of the senses and that sixth sense which includes the other five and transcends them as in the mind of a young scholar who has systematically deranged his sensibility.

Let the authors' motive be plainly stated: to adapt the language of conversation in the clueless media-saturated dumbed-down middle classes to the purposes of poetic pleasure. Readers accustomed to the gaudiness and inane phraseology of the poetasters who dominate the pages of literary journals will find much here that will seem awkward and strange; they will look round for "poetry" and will find none. Nor will they hear the bell that tolls for no one if not for him who declares that no man's island is better than no man's land as a place to make his stand and bend others' will to his wand. Such readers, while they are perusing this book, should ask themselves if the promised wafer of desire has met with the tongue of acceptance, and if the squeezed lemon of effort has expended itself in sugar and ice water with no need of a catalyst beyond a vigorous shaking of the beaker. They should consider further whether the resulting admixture has slaked the thirst in ample recompense for hours freely given and, if it has, has it not thereby for a moment blotted out the sneers of selfish men and all the dreary intercourse of daily life?

And if the answer to these questions is favorable to the authors' wishes, they should please consent to be pleased in spite of that most dreadful enemy of pleasure, our own preestablished codes of decision.

Table of Contents

Table of Contents

Many of these poems were written by David Lehman;
most of the others by that sestina lifer, Jim Cummins;
and one sestina was an invention of them both. Truth!
It's weird, but people often think a sestina is a knot
that's particularly difficult to tie—or untie. Be that
as it may, Dave and Jim think it's more like ringing a bell,

like Chuck Berry says Johnny B. Goode rings a bell—
you know, when it's done right. Now the David Lehman
way is a way uniquely his own, naturally, yet one that
contrasts with and complements sestinas by Jim Cummins;
& vice versa. (Seriously. No, really, pretty much. Or not.)
But at least they know that's one of the deals with truth:

it's not easy to show a reader, you know, "the whole truth."
Hey, sestinas convey more than the usual lyric "La belle
dame sans merci" shtick that pretty much goes for naught
when it comes to facts! Like, here's a fact: David Lehman
wrote "Big Hair," "End Note," "Sestina (for Jim Cummins),"
"The Prophet's Lantern," "The Hopeful Stakes," also that

tour de farce, "Operation Memory"—"merely" a sestina that
notes the problems which preclude our "knowing" "truth"!—
"A Valediction," "The 39 Steps," and suggested Jim Cummins
write "Monopolies," so Cummins could piss off Marvin Bell,
too. Done. (In his sestina for Jim Cummins, David Lehman
cracked wise about some poets' names & faces, but let's not

get into that.) "Secretariat" tied them both in a large knot—
they rode that poem together, got a big kick out of that.
But the "Masked Man" sestina is solely a David Lehman
dish, and like "Fast and Slow" and "Hotel Fiesta," tells truth
to various powers, as his "When he called the lawyer" and "The Bell
Telephone Hour" do. So were the rest written by Jim Cummins?

Certainly, this "t of c" was puzzled out by "Jim Cummins."
Pen for one's pen, Pan, pain, the sestina is such a naught-
y vehicle for naming, even if the name is only "Marvin Bell."
Let's see, "Salutation," "The Carey Treatment," and that
star, "The Old Constellation"—a quiet meditation on Truth
and Booty—could only come, and did, from David Lehman.

A Mississippi belle from Lake Forest wrote "To J.C. & D.L.,
etc.," while Billy W., that prince, helped Dave stretch the truth
in "Falstaff." And Jim Cummins wrote all the rest. Not not.

Salutation

Salutation

"I'll have to ask you to repeat that.
What did you say?" "No problem.
I said you're quite a young man to have
developed a case of amnesia as advanced
as yours." But he was thinking of writers
who bare their souls in popular magazines.

They confess their vices in such magazines
as *Spank, Ms. Fortune,* and *Beat That.*
That's the thing about ambitious middle-aged writers
who used to be young: each has a secret problem,
and if they confess it, they think it will advance
their careers. All believe they have

not been appreciated enough by lovers who have
cheated on them as by philistine editors of magazines
who commission out of hope and edit out of fear. The advance
on their next book is spent at lunch, and that
isn't funny. Six out of ten have a drinking problem.
But when was that a bar to their need to be writers?

To write a bestseller is every writer's
fantasy, and if you write three or four you'll have
retirement options beyond the usual. But look at the problems
standing between you and your modest goal of magazine
publication, a tenure-track appointment, and that
sexy partner you're trying to impress. Advance

praise has to be got from writers who've advanced
to the fore. To join the ranks of such writers
may, however, seem a less worthy goal now that
you've met the vain jerks who have
seized the means of production. Still, these problems
exist in order for you to solve them, and in your own magazine—

the apotheosis of a modern avant-garde magazine—
you may disdain to publish anyone save those with the most advanced
views, though that path may create yet more problems.
For often the most talented writers are not the writers
you'd like to have dinner with, have drinks with, even have
an elevator conversation with, about this, the other, or that.

To sum up: to publish a piece in that imaginary magazine,
you have to have an advanced case of something,
some marvelous incurable problem that will make you a writer.

Fling

Fling

He wanted to tell her the weekend idea was "neat,"
But he kept hearing himself repeat the word "funny."
She named the names of trees, flowers: *sycamore, tulip.*
He asked her who did she think she was, Gary Snyder?
Above the car, then over the hotel, the spring moon
Was full, orange. "This isn't just another fling,"

She said suddenly. "Don't dare think it's some fling."
The Jack Daniel's arrived, hers on the rocks, his neat.
"I didn't think that at all." Behind her, the moon
Looked away. She fretted. "I just—I feel funny."
Amazingly, it occurred to him something Gary Snyder
Once said was appropriate. He repeated it. "Tulips,"

She smiled back. "Let's take a walk through the tulips."
Later, they didn't make love. She was shy. Some fling,
He brooded. Did she really think he *liked* Gary Snyder—
That he, too, thought he had it all summed up in a neat
Little package? Funny, he groaned. Worse than funny.
I get it all right, for once: drinks, room, even the moon

Cooperates. How often can you count on a spring moon
Slipping through the sycamores, picking out the tulips
In the night air? She should feel romantic, not "funny"!
Lying next to her, he felt so restless, eager to fling
His body atop hers—seeking, yet in control, his need
Ascetic, sensual, yet poised—a suburban Gary Snyder....

In the dark, she teased: "Thinking about Gary Snyder?"
Then: "I'm not so shy now." He thought about the moon,
And a Grace Paley character who "liked his pussy neat."
Then she was touching him, needing him, her two lips
Soft flowers, emissaries of her body, gently ruffling
Against him, moving him, so powerfully it wasn't funny....

Afterward, they were awkward, shy, trying to be funny.
They couldn't get any more mileage out of Gary Snyder.
"Some fling," he said, and she flung back, "Some fling!"
But mostly they were quiet. Outside, the big yellow moon
Yawned. He made a mental note to send her some tulips.
She stared out the window, thinking about the word "neat."

He thought of how she'd fling her hair. And the moon....
It was *finito*. Next week he got a book by Gary Snyder
In the mail. That was funny. He sent her the tulips.

Sestina (for Jim Cummins)

Sestina

For Jim Cummins

In Iowa, Jim dreamed that Della Street was Anne Sexton's
twin. Dave drew a comic strip called the "Adventures of Whitman,"
about a bearded beer-guzzler in Superman uniform. Donna dressed like
    Wallace Stevens
in a seersucker summer suit. To town came Ted Berrigan,
saying, "My idea of a bad poet is Marvin Bell."
But no one has won as many prizes as Philip Levine.

At the restaurant, people were talking about Philip Levine's
latest: the Pulitzer. A toast was proposed by Anne Sexton.
No one saw the stranger, who said his name was Marvin Bell,
pour something into Donna's drink. "In the Walt Whitman
Shopping Center, there you feel free," said Ted Berrigan,
pulling on a Chesterfield. Everyone laughed, except T. S. Eliot.

I asked for directions. "You turn right on Gertrude Stein,
then bear left. Three streetlights down you hang a Phil Levine
and you're there," Jim said. When I arrived I saw Ted Berrigan
with cigarette ash in his beard. Graffiti about Anne Sexton
decorated the men's room walls. Beth had bought a quart of Walt Whitman.
"Come on," she said. "Back in the apartment I have vermouth and a jar of
    Marvin Bell."

You laugh, yet there is nothing inherently funny about Marvin Bell.
You cry, yet there is nothing inherently scary about Robert Lowell.
You drink a bottle of Samuel Smith's Nut Brown Ale, as thirsty as Walt Whitman.
You bring in your car for an oil change, thinking, this place has the aura of

Philip Levine.
Then you go home and write: "He kissed her Anne Sexton,
and she returned the favor, caressing his Ted Berrigan."

Donna was candid. "When the spirit of Ted Berrigan
comes over me, I can't resist," she told Marvin Bell,
while he stood dejected at the Xerox machine. Anne Sexton
came by to circulate the rumor that Robert Duncan
had flung his drink on a student who had called him Philip Levine.
The cop read him the riot act. "I don't care," he said, "if you're Walt Whitman."

Donna told Beth about her affair with Walt Whitman.
"He was indefatigable, but he wasn't Ted Berrigan."
The Dow Jones industrials finished higher, led by Philip Levine,
up a point and a half on strong earnings. Marvin Bell
ended the day unchanged. Analyst Richard Howard
recommended buying May Swenson and selling Anne Sexton.

In the old days, you liked either Walt Whitman or Anne Sexton,
not both. Ted Berrigan changed that just by going to a ballgame with
    Marianne Moore.
And one day Philip Levine looked in the mirror and saw Marvin Bell.

Monopolies: A Sentimental
Education

Monopolies: A Sentimental Education

In 1971 I went to study in Marvin Gardens,
but I probably should've gone to New York Avenue.
Some people wanted to see the Dead Man in jail
even then, but there was no justice. (Don was in Atlantic
City, I guess, taking a short break on the boardwalk.
He had that gambler's vision of Park Place.)

Marvin swore they wouldn't let him move to Park Place,
so he made his garage over into Marvin's Gardens.
There he could turn the recollections of any bored walk
into poems he tried to peddle on New York Avenue:
"Hashish? Suffering?" Walking along the Atlantic,
he felt sad and gray, and wise, like Oscar Wilde in jail.

I was writing "The Ballad of Reading (Railroad) Gaol"—
trying to be funny. I was from Porkopolis, "Pork Place";
I had to be funny. Funny was my ticket out, to the Atlantic
smorgasbord: bucks, tenure. The King of Marvin Gardens
wanted so awfully to be King of New York Avenue,
too: he'd swagger his tiny little torso into a Bard's walk,

around campus.... Don ground a butt into the boardwalk,
turned back to the blackjack game. "Go directly to jail,
Toto!" some Dorothy shouted on New York Avenue,
remembering Kansas. Marvin kept his little perks in place:
the young women trying to graduate from Marvin Gardens.
I watched a lot of movies—*Rules of the Game, L'Atalante*—

while classmates got poems published in the *Atlantic Monthly*. I took a job working for the Board of Walks; I had a mouth to feed. I wanted out of Marvin Gardens, badly. I'd spent most of my life in some sort of jail— too much Baltic Avenue, and not enough Park Place! I scanned the *Voice,* but the rents on New York Avenue

seemed so high: how could I afford New York Avenue? Something was pouring bean green over blue in the Atlantic— but it's not *me,* I swore over and over to the Park police. "Not *I,*" they smirked, as they hauled me off to Boardwalk, where they made me take the long way around to jail.... All the world's a stage, leaving at noon for Marvin Gardens.

I came home to Pork Place. I'd seen the lights of Boardwalk, New York Avenue; I'd smelled the gray tang of the Atlantic. But coveting is a jail. And your cellmate is Marvin Gardens.

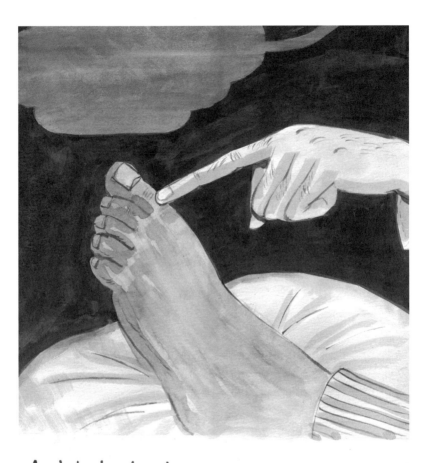

A Valediction:
Forbidding Mourning

A Valediction: Forbidding Mourning

You who are the reader
had an identity crisis, went to college,
went on strike,
but fell out with the movement
when someone started a fire in the library.
You were reading Rousseau at the time.

Hiking in the woods was your pastime.
You sat on a rock and wrote pages no reader
would see. Leaves were your library.
A congress of birds was your college.
They consoled you, told you to strike
up the band when down, play the scherzo movement

of a romantic symphony, and observe the movement
of water in the stream marking time.
You smoked unfiltered Lucky Strikes.
You defined a writer as a reader
who skipped classes in college,
spent nights in bars and days in the library.

One section of your ideal library
has books with blank pages. No movement
of men and arms can stand up to a college
of ideas: you believed that at the time.
You believed in the inalienable rights of the reader,
who could bring down poetry by going on strike.

Like a patient batter taking a first-pitch strike,
the professors assembled on the steps of Low Library,
and talked. Students perused *The Rousseau Reader.*
Some joined an underground movement
of philosophers committed to a new refutation of time.
The course you most wanted to take in college,

"Romanticism from Rousseau to Hitler," an old college
standby, gave way to a course on great strikes
in union history. Like a referee calling time,
the head librarian asked all to observe library
decorum and said that for the sestina movement
to get off the ground, we needed new readers.

Gather round, ye readers, nostalgic for college,
and the concepts of timeless truths beyond movements
of protestors striking poses in the photogenic library.

Thank You

Thank You

Kenneth noticed a man staring at breasts,
the way he, Kenneth, might look at an ass.
Kenneth felt a solidarity of need.
Then, as he walked along the city street,
a girl passed him, gazing between his legs:
she took his measure there, not in his face.

Kenneth was outraged. Rage reddened his face.
It didn't help that her quivering breasts
elicited no response between his legs.
He glanced backward at her quivering ass—
piglets under a scarf, on Houston Street!
Watching those retreating cheeks, his need

hardened—oh, friendly, long-understood need!—
setting off a music he could always face,
pulsing along a crowded New York street:
whenever he heard that music, breasts,
hips, thighs, came into play, not just ass.
As she vanished, Kenneth watched her legs:

he could get into just adoring legs....
He snapped to, shocked at how he'd bared his need
for all to see—he felt like such an ass!
Fly open, half-turned-around sweaty face
slipping over other hips and breasts,
flowing between him and the empty street:

he felt like something tossed onto the street.
He thought, incongruously, of frogs' legs—
then—equally insane—of chicken breasts!
Goddamn this growing old! Keeping one need
separate from the next—keeping one's face
pokered and cute—he *was* a horse's ass!

A girl walked by. His eyes locked on her ass.
I want to be in love! I want the street
to open like a painting of her face
in heat, he thought. *I need her lovely legs*
to wrap around me till they strangle need!
I need—I need—I need my mother's breasts!

That stopped him. *Did* he need his mother's breasts?
Thoughts swarmed him: Mom's legs, Mom's ass, Mom's face!
Edgar Allan Poe! he shouted, down the street.

Big Hair

Big Hair

Ithaca, October 1993: Jorie went on a lingerie
tear, wanting to look like a moll
in a Chandler novel. Dinner, consisting of three parts gin
and one part lime juice cordial, was a prelude to her hair.
There are, she said, poems that can be written
only when the poet is clad in black underwear.

But that's Jorie for you. Always cracking wise, always where
the action is, the lights, and the sexy lingerie.
Poems, she said, were meant to be written
on the run, like ladders on the stockings of a gun moll
at a bar. Jorie had to introduce the other poet with the fabulous hair
that night. She'd have preferred to work out at the gym.

She'd have preferred to work out with Jim.
She'd have preferred to be anywhere
but here, where young men gawked at her hair
and old men swooned at the thought of her lingerie.
"If you've seen one, you've seen the moll,"
Jorie said when asked about C. "Everything she's written

is an imitation of E." Some poems can be written
only when the poet has fortified herself with gin.
Others come easily to one as feckless as Moll
Flanders. Jorie beamed. "It happened here,"
she said. She had worn her best lingerie,
and D. made the expected pass at her. "My hair

was big that night, not that I make a fetish of hair,
but some poems must not be written
by bald sopranos." That night she lectured on lingerie
to an enthusiastic audience of female gymnasts and gin-
drinking males. "Utopia," she said, "is nowhere."
This prompted one critic to declare that, of them all,

all the poets with hair, Jorie was the fairest moll.
The *New York Times* voted her "best hair."
Iowa City was said to be the place where
all aspiring poets went, their poems written
on water, with blanks instead of words, a tonic
of silence in the heart of noise, and a vision of lingerie

in the bright morning—the lingerie to be worn by a moll
holding a tumbler of gin, with her hair
wet from the shower and her best poems waiting to be written.

Falstaff

Falstaff

"Look at that bum in the corner." "That's no bum, that's Harold Bloom."
If a tragic romance of uncles and aunts is the story of poetic influence,
he's the voice on the phone who talks without listening, a lightning rod of anxiety.
The rest of us are in prison, but the walls are not made of words, and misprision
will not bend the bars that keep us from our freedom, as the new canon
keeps cadets in the dark on the charms of Hamlet or Falstaff.

Some have greatness thrust upon them. Then there is Falstaff,
asleep under a tree, indifferent to the charms of flowers in bloom.
Some dream of glory in combat. But he has heard the cannons
roar. The noise made him cherish the more the influence
of sack in the conduct of man's affairs. Not subject to misprision
is this self-evident truth: that we live and die alone, with anxiety

our common lot. Consider Nym, whose anxiety
was jealousy, a humor his master Falstaff
found humorous. Poor deluded Nym misread
his Mistress, believed her more constant than Mrs. Bloom.
Then under the broken-hearted influence
of too much Eastcheap Sack, he broke the canon-

ic law and robbed the Church (and took a non-
stop flight, anon, to the gallows). Anxiety
is the humor of our age, an influence
for the worse. For Dr. Bloom that old bum Falstaff
is the only cure. To be human, says Bloom,
is to be Hal, not Henry—a king mistaken

for a man by scholarly fools in whose misreading
the play's the site of a battle pitting Jill's canon
against Jack's, with Leo's old vision of a New Bloom-
usalem receding as fast as anxiety
will allow. And therefore do we turn to Falstaff
with our flags at half-staff under the influence

of parents, teachers, and stars. The influence
of Falstaff is the will to live, to escape the prison
of our days, not to praise them. Falstaff
is all men, potentially (except Milton). "Yet the canon's
contradictions may doom it," Jack said, radiating anxiety.
"And well they should!" said Jill: "Doom to Bloom!"

Yet when midnight chimes, 'tis the influence of Jack's canon
that makes Miss Priss unbosom her anxiety
in the giant arms of Falstaff, conceiving Bloom.

The Bell Telephone Hour Sestina

The Bell Telephone Hour Sestina

A rabbi, a minister, and a priest were watching
the movie *Our Hitler.* "What do you mean *our?*"
the rabbi asked. The minister said, "Maybe
you should say *her.*" The priest, summoned on the phone,
wondered who *she* was. "Saved by the bell,"
I thought, sneaking out the back, escaping into the city.

I'd grown up near here but could barely recognize the city.
I moved furtively, knowing everyone was watching.
I looked for familiar landmarks, a cracked Liberty Bell,
the gravestone of an American president. It was the hour
between dusk and nightfall. Not a phone
booth in sight. Was I lost? Maybe,

but too proud to ask for directions. "There may be
trouble ahead," I hummed, turning the city
into a newspaper office. My old job! "Rilke's on the phone,"
the boss said, looking quizzical. When he wasn't watching,
a dozen sonnets had landed on his desk. "Just our
luck," he sighed. "Now there won't be room for the Bell

& Howell scandal." He seemed close to tears. (Lunch at Hell
& Bowel, the local slop joint, hadn't helped.) Oh, baby. Maybe
their spin doctors were winning the propaganda war while our
vaunted investigative team sat on its hands at the city
desk. Heartburn. His staff stood around idly watching
the old fart let off steam. It was then that the phone

rang a second time, making everyone jump. "Hold the phone.
Did anyone here order take-out from Taco Bell?"
"I did," a girl said, "while *he* was watching
Our Hitler in the movies." People gasped. "This may be
the recognition scene I had escaped into the city
to avoid," I thought. But the lateness of the hour

meant that it would never arrive, and I, feeling dour,
figured why not and picked up the phone
to call the dead man one last time. "O City, city,"
the dumbbell moaned. You could hear the funeral bell
toll in the little village where he grew up. "Maybe
I should have stayed in the movie house, watching

our soldiers fight theirs, while the world was watching
with one eye closed." Right. And maybe help was a phone
call away. In my mind, bells rang in New York City.

Collegiality

Collegiality

A man takes off his glasses, after a hard day
at work, squeezes his nose, and rubs his eyes
so hard he scoops out an eyeball by mistake.
He cups it gently, still attached to his face,
goes out to the car, realizes he can't do it,
calls 911. At the hospital, they prep his head.

His eyeball floats in a dish next to his head.
What the hell have I done? "What a day!"
he jokes with the orderlies. "Never forget it!"
They don't respond. Tears fill up his eyes.
Oh, god, I can't cry! He wants to wipe his face,
but he's afraid. *Dear God, make it a mistake,*

he prays. *Please make it all a sad mistake....*
Then he's out, and they start in on his head.
"I don't even look," says one, "at the face.
If I thought about it, it would ruin my day!"
Another nods. Above his mask, his eyes
signal agreement. "Why I continue to do it,

I haven't the foggiest! Each day, I feel it:
the constant ritual address of mistake."
"Yes! *Yes!*" exclaims a third. Her eyes,
too, were sending signals from her head.
"Oh, it's so true—every day! Every *day!*
Oh, God, I feel it, too—face after face

of derision, carelessness, panic—my face
begins to mirror theirs—oh, yes, I *feel* it!"
The others stare at her. "It's quite a day,"
the first one resumes, watchful, "no mistake
about that." The second one nods his head.
The third one blushes, dropping her eyes.

Suddenly, as if the eyeball had eyes,
it squirts between them, slips off the face,
distending floorward from that sad head,
until a soft sucking "pop" severs it.
The garrulous one then makes a mistake
she'll live with the rest of her days—

more than a mistake: she steps on it. Her face
distends, eyes popping out of *her* head—
the others call her Big Foot to this day.

The World's Trade

The World's Trade

"No ideas but in things" is an idea,
after all, and not simply that a thing
is better than its idea. *No world
but mine* is what that ploy suggests: the self
as banner of some god. The worn-out face
of your god now must bow down to my god.

In our beginning, Jews invented God.
He broke bread, laughed with them, a new idea
about the human world. And this god's face
was mild yet stern, insisting on one thing:
"God" is just the way we hear the self—
our first allegiance must be to *this* world.

That brilliant trope was lost upon the world,
which then made sure the Jews devised a god
of war, a callow god, with which the self
identified, became the false idea
of power over things. The privileged *thing*
replaced the glory of the human face.

To be a Christian *is* to wear "God's face"—
a nightmare god of greed, who knows the world
belongs to him by right. The measured thing
behind the mask—the red hole crying "God"
and pillage camouflaged as Idea—
abstracts us all in service to "Himself."

The other spawn, Islam, deludes itself
a man is strong to loathe a woman's face.
Its vain men robe themselves in the idea
they are powerful and make the world
veil itself, too, before their righteous god.
Two "faiths," revealing no idea, thing,

but arrogance, hatred: ideas, things.
Eliot thought abstraction frayed the self
into false premises, one of them "God."
Before Plato, man's face was still a face,
not a marker played out to trick the world.
Now love is marketed, mere idea

that faces down opposed ideas of self.
Men blow up things built to a different god,
displace death onto Christ, Allah, the world.

The Prophet's Lantern

The Prophet's Lantern

What's new?
The question implies a possibility:
that the old saw wasn't true,
the one that says there's nothing
new under the sun.
The prophet rests in the shade.

Not black but a dark shade
of blue is the shade in which the new
growth, protected from the sun,
tests the possibility
that the prophet's vision of nothing
could not come true.

The prophet knows true
north is the direction of a shade
after death when nothing
further can be done, no new
remedy can revive the possibility
of new light from an ancient sun.

In the glare of the midday sun
things that were true
at night grow faint. The possibility
of love's warmth in a cool shade
is what's needed: something new,
not just a reiteration of nothing.

"The sun shone on the nothing
new," he wrote. Blank was the sun,
the masses quit the church, and new
pigeons ate stale bread. The true
isn't equal to the good; there's a shade
of difference between the possibility

that judgment is futile and the possibility
that it can't be evaded, as nothing
in our destiny can be. Linger in the shade,
we may as well. We cannot bear too much sun
if the one thing that is true
is that everything is possible, nothing new.

Yet news travels fast. Nothing lasts.
The possibility of love among the shades
remains as true as when the sun was new.

Fantasia with Tragg

Fantasia with Tragg

Tragg folded the band of his shorts, slid his hand
down his crotch, softly but firmly cupping his balls,
rubbed his fingers rapidly over the head of his dick.
He squeezed his balls gently, let his fingers slip down
to the base of the prostate, felt them play like a tongue
on the small nut, as he sank into the throes of memory....

Maybe that had been his first pun, he thought. *Mammary*....
He imagined his mother's big firm breast, his tiny hand
searching for a nipple, then licking it with his tongue,
to get it into his mouth and suck the milk. His balls
tightened as he twisted around, humping up and down
in his chair, caressing, manipulating his stiff dick.

He lowered his head, wanting to suck his own dick.
He stared at its face: blind, infantile, without memory.
It stared back. He remembered the first girl to go down
on it, how she'd kissed it, then taken it into her hand,
pulling it into her mouth, all the while stroking his balls
with her other hand, laving him eagerly with her tongue....

Fascinated by her mobile mouth, its cat-quick tongue,
he forgot what was required of him, and his dick
sagged like an ancient breast.... She'd rubbed his balls
as one rubs the wrists of the faint, as if the memory
of life quickens the blood, or the laying on of hands
gets a rise out of the dead. But he had fallen down,

through the circle of her grip, past his shorts, down
past his balls even, down, down, his dick now the tongue
of his vertical smile, down from her mouth and hands
to someplace between his legs, a wagging tail of a dick....
Damn! he swore as he snapped out of it: the memory
of that humiliation dogged him. He rubbed his aching balls,

sat up.... Say, what if it were he himself who licked balls?
He conjured up a stock hunk, who got him to go down
on him, sweet mammaries of women just sweet memories
now, as he drove a man crazy with his mouth, tongue....
When he turned over, offering him his ass, his hard dick
shot wild sticky spurts of semen, onto his shorts, hands....

He'd use his tongue like a dog's, to lick his own dick
and balls if he could. Instead he just stretched his hand
down to the Kleenex box. And chuckled. *Mammary....*

Hamilton Loses His
Foot Cherry

Hamilton Loses His Foot Cherry

He wanted to make love to her feet,
but he didn't trust her. He was afraid
of exposure. What if he revealed to her
he needed this most—and she said no?
Offered a blow job instead? He'd die.
But what if Della half-lowered her eyes

and said yes? He half-lowered his eyes....
All night she'd let him stare at her feet,
watching the fire in the fireplace die,
barely speaking, each of them afraid
to break the mood, the spell. "Oh, no,"
she said at last (disappointment in her

voice, he was sure), "it's so late!" Her
eyes darted a look at his, but his eyes
slid away. Then the damned panic. "No,
wait," he blurted, staring at Della's feet
so hard he was making himself afraid....
But he let the moment pass, die—

and with it hopes for the evening die,
too: next minute, she was brushing her
hair, talking about a cab. "I'm afraid
I've kept you up"—staring into his eyes.
Mocking him? He shuffled his feet.
"So have I kept you...up?" "Oh, no,"

he laughed, hating himself, her. "No—"
He heard something in his voice die.
"What?" She waited. "These?" Her feet,
curled under her as she'd brushed her
hair, slid toward him. He shut his eyes.
Della said quietly, "Don't be afraid...."

He was petrified, so he said, "Afraid?
Who's afraid?" Della shook her head no,
smiling softly. She half-lowered her eyes.
"Yes," she whispered. He wanted to die,
but found himself kneeling before her,
mouthing like a madman her naked feet.

Eyes wide in the dark. "We're just afraid
to die, darling," Della sighed. "You know
how it is." Her feet were cold on his feet.

Encounter (after Lorca)

Encounter (after Lorca)

"You want to be part of the night—
only you psycho white boys want that.
But we *are* part of the night—*black*
night. Blackest night you ever gonna know."
"Oh, give me a big break. That shit"—
Paul gripped his pepper canister—"is so history."

"Maybe this time *you're* history,"
His Motherfucker smirked, and this time the night
really did seem to back his shit.
Paul felt a sudden spasm of fear that
he sure didn't want this clown to know
about. "Maybe it's *your* black

ass that's over with"—but Paul said "black"
with way too much history
to get Mistah Gangsta rattled. "Oh, I know"—
black arms wide, pretending to beseech the night—
"Lord, how I know!" He knew Paul knew that
Paul had blinked first. He also knew Paul's shit

was almost in his pants. "Sheee-yit!"
Paul said, bravely—a little black
humor in God knows what desperation that
he might still finesse it. "History
be doomed to repeat you," the Other intoned, "every night
you don't listen to what it know..."

God knows I don't know
shit, Paul prayed, pointing the spray: "Try this shit
for size!" But Hip Hop had reached up into the night
and brought his hand back down with a black
blade in it. Oh, the funny twists history
takes as it smashes into you—that

blade stuck in the black briefcase that
Paul flung up. They danced a dance, you know,
the next few seconds of their history—
almost shy and embarrassed, shit
on their shoes. The handle had black
tape on it. Its owner bolted off into the night.

One's history can end at night. Some black
or white shit says it's over, and that's
that. *I'm lucky,* Paul grinned. *God know.*

Tiresias Mason

Tiresias Mason

You learn how to be a man from your father.
Your mother teaches you how to be a woman.
You have to fear becoming an old man
before you'll take on the wiles of the mother—
her movements, gestures, the way her face
suddenly, at odd moments, becomes your face.

Turns out that old adage about saving face
was really about saving the face of the father.
His was the look you wanted on your face
whenever you'd realize you were a woman.
Those moments shocked you—and your mother,
who'd assumed you'd turn out to be a man.

But it's not that you haven't ended up a man:
mornings you shave, staring into a man's face;
you have the proper attitude toward your mother.
You just don't want to be a man like your father,
and the best way to do that is to be a woman.
The first time you saw this happen in your face,

it scared you; your hand flew up to your face.
Not only did you have the cunning of a man,
now you also had the guile of a woman.
You look into the mirror at your new face,
one begun the night it surprised your father
humping a blanket that turned into your mother.

How could the bastard do that to your mother?
And why had you never seen this in her face?
What was it you saw next day in your father?
A look that told you he was the better man?
And what do you think he saw in your face?
Did he know then that you were a woman?

You repressed that morning in the way a woman
might repress an impractical love for a man.
When he's around, you can see it in her face—
her Don't-trust-him-but-still-love-him face.
Your father never thought of you as a man.
It was natural you'd try to seduce your father.

First you showed your father your "mother" face;
but then you showed him your other face,
the sly face a man wears when he's a woman.

Home Alone

Home Alone

"'Fuck me? Fuck me? Fuck you, you fucking fuck!'"
Della closed the book, finished for the night.
"What's that?" he called. *"Death of a Salesman?*
That Willy guy? What was his name? Willy—"
"Loman," she answered. "On the totem pole!
His totem pole was only *average."*

She giggled. Ham's pole was only "average,"
too, which made him nervous before a fuck.
She liked that in a man. A CNN poll
once canvassed fifty "ladies of the night"
to see how they'd rank a man's "Willy"—
a priest, a pool boy, and a car salesman

topped the whores' ratings—the used car salesman's
dick, especially, "above average."
He yelled, "Not funny!" "So how's *your* Willy?"
she yelled back. (He washed it before each fuck.)
"Nilly? Don't towel off too well!" The night
grimaced outside, quite like a totem pole.

"Ha ha," he said, as he lay down, his pole
most unpole-like. "I think I read *Salesman*
in school," he said. "Stayed up all one night."
She snickered, "Raising your 'D' average,
no doubt." He winced, but played along. "Fuck
you," he said. "You wish," she said. "Or your Willy

wishes." She reached down, grabbed it. "Hey, Willy!"
Della singsonged. "Are you a *token* pole?"
"Fuck you! You think that makes me want to fuck?"
"I wasn't reading *Death of a Salesman*—"
"You make me feel like Dame Edna Everage—!"
"You *look* like Dame Edna Everage tonight!

And that was Mamet, not Miller, tonight!"
This wasn't going well. Mocking Willy
could mean watching the Dow Jones average
crawl by, followed by sports. "Hey, guy, some *pole!*"
she breathed, as if she meant it—no salesman
blew smoke like Della when she craved a fuck.

Tonight, Leno was kissing Dame Everage.
"My Willy-pole.... Come here, you wittle fuck!"
Ham turned away. "So call the car salesman!"

The Thirty-Nine Steps

The 39 Steps

Logic can take you only *to* the border, not over it.
I am sad. But I have the protection of speech.
The rest is only the first time I saw a cross
Around the neck of a uniformed girl my age
In the public library, making her strange and very,
Very beautiful. The rest consists of youth's

Refusals to take anything seriously except youth's
Reluctance to grow up and be done with it.
You are happier. Shyly, you have come to the very
Edge of finding out. But as the sergeant's brave speech
Was forgotten, minutes after, by the soldiers who came of age
During their first tour of the distant hill, the one with the cross

On top of it, so some hypothetical "he" may now see that same cross
As the genius of Christianity as art. With an innocence most youths
His age were likely to conceal, he wanted to be age-
Less rather than adult, and wondered if it
Was true, that the words of the senator's splendid speech
Meant nothing whatsoever. Did it change the chill he felt in his very

Heart? Perhaps he was the only one paying very
Close attention. These graduation ceremonies were a cross,
Usually, of the stupidly funny and the stupidly boring. The speech
Of formal gibberish, the inaccurate notion that all youths
Become men at precisely the same instant, the way it
All seemed as opaque and foolishly friendly as an adage

Or an order issued by a mother. "Act your age,"
Mine still says to me, and at twenty-eight I'm still not very
Clear as to what that means. Does it
Imply, for example, a mandatory choosing at every which cross-
Roads? Yes, tell me about the prerogatives of youth's
Decline into maturity. That would make a pretty speech,

And stripped of sermon, pep talk, and speech,
You and I are likely to feel naked, of indeterminate age,
And indistinguishable. This is the point of youth's
Indifference: the first of any new series always seems the very
Last of the series that preceded it
Into oblivion. So it must have seemed to the original cross-

Carrier before it was finished. Yet the youths
Still listened, as though to a very solemn speech,
Listened and wept, dragging the years across the backs of their age.

Operation Memory

Operation Memory

We were smoking some of this knockout weed when
Operation Memory was announced. To his separate bed
Each soldier went, counting backwards from a hundred
With a needle in his arm. And there I was, in the middle
Of a recession, in the middle of a strange city, between jobs
And apartments and wives. Nobody told me the gun was loaded.

We'd been drinking since early afternoon. I was loaded.
The doctor made me recite my name, rank, and serial number when
I woke up, sweating, in my civvies. All my friends had jobs
As professional liars, and most had partners who were good in bed.
What did I have? Just this feeling of always being in the middle
Of things, and the luck of looking younger than fifty.

At dawn I returned to draft headquarters. I was eighteen
And counting backwards. The interviewer asked one loaded
Question after another, such as why I often read the middle
Of novels, ignoring their beginnings and their ends. When
Had I decided to volunteer for intelligence work? "In bed
With a broad," I answered, with locker-room bravado. The truth was, jobs

Were scarce, and working on Operation Memory was better than no job
At all. Unamused, the judge looked at his watch. It was 1970
By the time he spoke. Recommending clemency, he ordered me to go to bed
At noon and practice my disappearing act. Someone must have loaded
The harmless gun on the wall in Act I when
I was asleep. And there I was, without an alibi, in the middle

Of a journey down nameless, snow-covered streets, in the middle
Of a mystery—or a muddle. These were the jobs
That saved men's souls, or so I was told, but when
The orphans assembled for their annual reunion, ten
Years later, on the playing fields of Eton, each unloaded
A kit bag full of troubles, and smiled bravely, and went to bed.

Thanks to Operation Memory, each of us woke up in a different bed
Or coffin, with a different partner beside him, in the middle
Of a war that had never been declared. No one had time to load
His weapon or see to any of the dozen essential jobs
Preceding combat duty. And there I was, dodging bullets, merely one
In a million whose lucky number had come up. When

It happened, I was asleep in bed, and when I woke up,
It was over. I was thirty-eight, on the brink of middle age,
A succession of stupid jobs behind me, a loaded gun on my lap.

The Carey Treatment

The Carey Treatment

Still there will be your desire, and her desire,
and his desire, and their desire. —Kenneth Fearing

There was his desire and there was her desire
and then there was their desire, and the doctor
wasn't wearing a name tag. It was a boy.
He was nineteen, wounded, in pain,
needing morphine. Someone in the hospital
had killed her and made it look like an accident.

What was the difference between an accident
and a mistake? It had something to do with desire.
The one place I don't want to die is the hospital,
where love is the nurse and death the doctor,
and pleasure the dream of an antidote to pain
and a lull in the conflict between girl and boy.

There was only one thing they knew about the boy—
his birth came about as an accident.
There was his desire and there was her pain
and then there was his pain and her desire.
Not every illness requires a doctor
to diagnose it in the ward of a hospital.

The greatest murder mystery ends in the hospital
where the star witness is the former boy
genius in the wheelchair who wrote his doctoral
thesis on the importance of accidents
in military history. In youth, desire;

in age the desperate avoidance of pain
was his theme. But she specialized in terminal pain
and she had the night shift at the hospital.
The proximity of death aroused her desire
and the look in her eyes told the boy
he could safely proceed. It was no accident;
they learned the rules of cause and effect playing doctor.

There are soldiers who have a fear of doctors
and old, infirm citizens who seem immune to pain.
It is the rare driver who has never had an accident.
It is the rare mother who gives birth not in the hospital
but in a speeding taxi. It was a boy
whose arrival gratified the aging couple's desire.

He had the desire but not the discipline to become a doctor.
Yet the boy survived his addiction to pain
and recovered from the accident in the hospital.

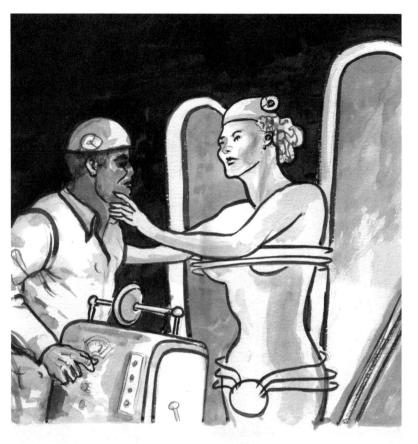

The Body Is The Flower

The Body Is the Flower

So bondage is a big part of it, after all—
that old art of rendering a lover submissive:
a tactic, a strategy. Denying somebody's body
the power to move denies that body the power
to be believed. Isn't that what's so sexual?
The intimate plea? The fear you can't go back?

Until your lover throws you over on your back.
Maybe a woman becomes a man, then. After all,
it's the head games that conjure up the sexual:
which one agrees, this time, to be submissive;
which one straps on the fetishes, the powers,
we make to make the body yield up the body....

O the rendering, the surrendering of the body!
We so much want to go back, all the way back....
You stand before a mirror, naked, the power
of someone's eyes, words, erasing you, the all
you claim to be. Belief can be so submissive:
desire, not truth. But being believed is sexual

vantage: the crying out, the echo, the sexual
need you never knew could subjugate the body....
So you cry out at the idea of her, submissive,
yes, her hands your hands, *yes,* leading you back,
her voice your voice, *o god,* eyes lips cunt all
mirroring, *yes,* the glory, *o god yes,* the power....

Later, you wipe off the remnants of the power
with Kleenex. When you get down to the sexual
level, you get sexually leveled, that's all:
doesn't discipline make a believer of the body?
You whisper no name but hers in the going back.
Tomorrow, it will be her turn to be submissive:

the ties that bind render you both submissive.
You'll need her to believe your plea, her power;
she'll need you to escort her all the way back,
before the life alongside this life, her body
alongside yours: ravenous, indifferent, sexual.
There, anything might happen, anything at all,

if all you need is to be believed. The power
of the sexual plea masquerades as the submissive
act. The body is the flower of the going back.

Portrait of a Lady

Portrait of a Lady

"You ought to see a great many men.... You ought to see
as many as possible, so as to get used to them." "Used
to them?" Isabel repeated with that solemn stare. "Why,
I'm not afraid of them. I'm as used to them as the cook
to the butcher-boys." "Used to them, I mean, so as to
despise them. That's what one comes to with most of them."

How she loved that passage, even though one of "them"
had written it. But James was different: he could see
how women think—and how most men aren't able to.
She was waiting for her own Gilbert, who would use
her differently. It was just pride: Isabel would cook,
take in laundry, before she'd cave, and she knew why—

often, she marveled that Henry James knew why.
She flipped on a movie, a sci-fi flick called *Them*—
radioactive ants, antennae waving like an Italian cook
on *Lucy*—and wondered why her Gilbert couldn't see
her inner Isabel, the one that counted, before he used
her body to relieve himself (and to be fair, her, too).

She felt small hairy arms waving inside her, too—
boss at the office, lover at the orifice—why
was it with these guys you always felt so used?
She jumped as the television screamed, "It's *them!*
Oh my God! *Them!*" She looked up in time to see
flame-throwers roar, segmented bodies cook....

She goes to the kitchen, fixes herself a drink, says,
No, I won't be like my mother, pours it out, waits.
She walks into the bedroom, pulls a pink vibrator
out of a drawer, hidden there beneath her underwear.
She lies on her stomach, pushing the vibes into her
from behind. She groans his name when she comes....

She likes to watch him while he makes her come.
If only he'd watch back.... He starts to look, says
he wants to, head bowed. But no, he listens to her,
then withdraws, idly flicking her nipple weights.
He's grateful: she makes him wear her underwear.
Sometimes, she makes him take the vibrator—

She capped her Mont Blanc pen. She could see
"Gil" on the porch. Oh, she was used to them—
who knew why? She drained her rum-and-coke.

Sestina: When he
called the lawyer

Sestina: When he called the lawyer.

When the doctor told her.
Most women would have said.
She smoked, puffed, inhaled him.
In those days the worst.
To want to marry him.
She stood there waiting for.

He quoted it wrong for.
One man's meat is another.
She: "I wouldn't tell him."
He wasn't drunk, he said.
He reassured her the worst.
Lonely, she dreamed of him.

But it wasn't about him.
The money wasn't meant for.
Their luck went from worse.
Everyone came home when mother.
So he said, she said.
She could have kissed him.

There was no mistaking him.
But was it really him?
Things happened after they said.
If they were free for.
Why get into a lather.
Best-case scenario or worst.

If you can say worse.
She felt like slapping him.
Look at it from her.
The fight was between him.
She gave him what for.
"That's not what I said."

"I loved you," he said.
When worst comes to worst.
Give her three or four.
Give my love to him.
(Everyone loves him except him.)
She had to console her.

She didn't know who her.
Worse, tell him who said.
It was good for him.

End Note

End Note

For Victor Cruz

I hitched my wagon to a whale in the clouds
Obscuring the star in the turbulent sky
I'd had my sights set on. You were my friend.
You understand. To say *I tried* is to say
I failed if meaning is to language as the end-
Game is to chess. Knight takes pawn, check and mate.

This knight was in possession of a fortune, in want of a mate,
In the post-pill, pre-AIDS era. His head was in the clouds,
But the rest of him was down below, enjoying the desired end
Of his wooing. "Contemplating a flying visit to the sky
Is safer than walking in the south Bronx, but if, say,
You were to come along, I'd chance it," he told his girlfriend,

Who, when they became lovers, didn't stop being his friend.
Her name was Marie. Her role was that of the first mate
In the story of a mutiny. Loyal to the captain, she would say
Something wonderfully cryptic about clouds
As instruments of divination in the reddening sky
Into which the two of them walked, hand in hand. The End.

As for the pawn: In art the means justify the ends.
In ethics they do not. In the Bronx, the friends
Of the fallen street fighter gathered to fill the sky
With an exaltation of larks. Far from the stalemate
In the killing fields, I could see the clouds
Of indifference. A man died in the arms of his fiancée.

The stunned girl feared she would never get to say
The sacred words at the altar. She wanted to end
This game of trial-and-error. Her ex-lover was a cloud
In trousers, a dead ringer for the hero of *The American Friend*
At the Thalia. Now again she was without a mate
And she was beautiful. Was the fault in the sky

Or in herself that she was single? "In the sky,"
Replied the mirror with her yen for lost causes and passé
Passions. In the zoo she watched the monkeys mate
And wished it could be that simple. The end
Of the affair had left her bereft, without a friend
She could talk to, afraid of crowds, lost in clouds

Of smoke, clouds of witness in an unforgiving sky.
The whole experience was an essay in friendship. My friend,
My mate. Forever may you live where memories end.

Romantic Love

Romantic Love

Love doesn't go away.
You can't tell love no,
then expect it to vanish,
as if you never have a thought
again of limbs in motion,
bodies at rest. Love,

once there, is always love,
always there. Turn away
the lover's great emotion,
his body chafes, as *No*
chafes a child. Then a thought
of her, and worlds vanish,

as a child's hurt will vanish,
soothed by a *Yes* of love.
Yeats said he had a thought
of loving in the old high way
but Maud Gonne said no,
with a quick hand motion,

a quick impatient motion,
that caused his heart to vanish.
But love didn't vanish, no,
it became a paradigm of love:
he made a map of the way
we become ourselves. The thought

the sheer amount of thought,
he diverted from his emotion
staggers the mind. The Way
is a way to vanish
from the grasp of Love,
a way of saying no

that is the opposite of no.
The unsettling thought
there might be a higher love
engenders an emotion
we want to vanish.
The way is only the way;

we know thought is emotion.
We long to vanish in love;
that way is our way.

The Hopeful Stakes
(Saratoga)

The Hopeful Stakes (Saratoga)

The odds-on favorite to cop the $50,000 purse, Lil's Lad,
was a late scratch. The smart money moved to Trafalgar,
but I put my twenty bucks on Pyramid's Peak
at 12-1. Barbara, who knows horses, said Risky Buy
could surprise. For sentimental reasons, Tom picked Oro de Mexico.
(Think Acapulco Gold.) And you know who won? Diligence.

Back to reality. "It's a question of due diligence,"
Herb Vienna was saying. He didn't look glad
to see me. "Have you considered running guns to Mexico?"
The English are forever saying goodbye Piccadilly, farewell Trafalgar
Square, and I'm English, and so to Mexico I went to buy
worthless pieces of paper from a military man who didn't speak

English. I knew no Spanish, so we got along fine. The peak
of our partnership was a scam we planned with amazing diligence
and pulled off with aplomb in Acapulco. By the time we said goodbye
we had made a pile. I took off. He took up with a local lad.
That was why Herb was chewing me out behind his desk in Trafalgar.
My orders had been to bring the chap back from Mexico.

Nor law nor duty but glory had brought me to Mexico.
There was a woman there. We were both at the peak
of our sexual power. Unlike Nelson at Trafalgar,
I wasn't about to pay for all this glory with my life, diligence
in the preservation of which is a virtue. Like the masked lad
of Incan legend, I would use the loot to buy

the freedom of one hundred serfs. Yes, thanks to my bi-
cameral brain, I could suppose that Mexico's
War of Independence was my real reason for coming, I, a lad
straight out of a Robert Louis Stevenson novel, at the peak
of youth. Though I favored pacifism over belligerence,
war was inevitable, and I longed for a battle decisive as Trafalgar

to show my mettle. At the agency's offices, near Trafalgar,
they gave me maps, a pistol, a poison pellet, money to buy
respect but not love from the defeated enemy, whose diligence
in observing the secret treaty would be the key to Mexico
and its plunder: gold and jewels of which pirates speak
with wonder. But I am not now the man I was. I am still the lad

who had to choose between rival dreams of Mexico and Trafalgar,
a lad who knew the difference between diligence
and a risky bilateralism at the peak of the Cold War.

...and turning for home,
it was Secretariat!

...and turning for home, it was Secretariat!

I was supposed to meet Monica, my secretary, at
Three o'clock: where was she? I felt like a ruffian,
Standing in the infield, watching the wind whirl away
Lost tickets. A policeman approached. A citation
Of some sort? No, he tipped his cap. "Sir Barton?"
He inquired, most respectfully. "Yes," I affirmed—

"What is it?" "Just routine," the cop affirmed.
I felt like a low-ranking diplomat at the UN Secretariat
Accused of spying for Belgium. Would the real Sir Barton
Avoid his inquisitor's eyes as I did? No ruffian,
He, but a master of codes, ciphers, and encrypted citations
In fortune cookies. ("Autumn comes, goes, and whirls away.")

I cleared my head.... That world was world's away
From this one. The policeman's handshake was a firm,
Live thing. He pulled an envelope from his book of citations,
Then blushed. "Sir, I—I spoke with your secretary at—"
Scrawled across pink flowers, in Monica's ruffian
Hand, was what the young man pointed to: "Sir Barton."

"Huh," I said thoughtfully. What was Monica doing at Sir Barton,
My estate, where I go to get away from the social whirl? Away—
I needed to whirl away. Having no choice but to play the ruffian,
I slugged the cop and ran. My masculinity thus affirmed,
I felt good. But there was still the question of my secretary. At
A loss I looked up her name in the index. Two citations

For cigar smuggling. Wait, what's this? A third citation—
A monograph! Horrified, I read: *The Life and Times of Sir Barton!*
The scamp! The exploiter! Hastily, I cell-phoned the Secretariat.
"Adlai!" I shouted, "Adlai!"—but I watched my words whirl away,
As I realized, with a shock, Adlai was dead. I was alone, a firm-
Ament of pain my sole sky. I was, at last, one of the roughs. "Ian!"

I said, catching sight of James Bond's creator. In the rough and
Tumble of life, the man stood erect, in an obvious state of excitement.
What the cop had intimated about Monica was true, he affirmed.
Indeed he had just spent a delightful day with her at Sir Barton.
All of them were in on the plot. It was, well, an LA way
Of doing business. Everything was for sale, even the name "Secretariat."

After his recitation of the specials—including orange roughy and
Pepsi—the waiter whirled away. Sir Barton sighed. The rather, ah, *firm*
Haunches of the lad reminded him of that great warrior, Secretariat.

Fast and Slow Sestina

Fast and Slow Sestina

For Joanna Yas of Open City

The woman he didn't marry did her best to rescue
the professor's son who worshiped Voltaire
and sipped no liquor nor broke his fast
until the dream blonde (who may look dumb
but isn't) smiled as if he were the man
destined to make her his wife.

And he wondered: Has the magic vanished from *wife,*
that once magical word? Is rescue
from the wedded state needed by the majority of man-
and-wife teams this side of the Quai Voltaire?
Those who know the right answer play dumb
and distrust people who talk too much too fast.

My mother told her daughters not to walk too fast.
What sort of man would want a fast-walking wife?
My girlfriend's fuck-me look said, "I may look dumb,
but rings of fire encircle me, whom you must rescue
and bring home to your own backyard (as Voltaire
wrote in *Candide*) to earn your status as an alpha man,

high in testosterone but brainier than the typical man
you meet in erotic cyberspace." Man, she talked fast.
Meanwhile, I told the driver to take us to 17 Quai Voltaire
where a party in honor of a theater producer's trophy wife
was in progress. The toastmaster said he "came not to rescue
Calpurnia but to praise her." No one got it. Boy, did he look dumb.

But think of the eloquence achieved by some who stay dumb
as Cordelia does when a more selfish woman or man
would write glib sonnets of praise rather than recuse
themselves from the proceedings going on at a pace too fast
for anyone to follow. The man who would go home to his wife
had best stay there, in the living room, and read Voltaire.

And he wondered: How many who walk on the Quai Voltaire
think of Voltaire? So much for posterity: fame is dumb;
the man who would achieve greatness must first get a wife,
and love her, and breed a gang of kids with her, and be a man
and not whine when things begin to go downhill fast
as they always do in the end and you wait in vain to be rescued.

Only religion promises rescue, and about religion you feel as Voltaire
did: skeptical but nostalgic for the dumb masses, the steadfast
believers, who persist in joining hands today as man and wife.

David Lehman and Jim
Cummins Run Poems for the
CIA in Nicaragua

David Lehman & Jim Cummins Run Poems for the CIA in Nicaragua

I look at David. He looks at me. We both look at "Rimbaud,"
a CIA stud who writes poems and looks a lot like Sly Stallone.
He is wearing his Edgar Allan Poe fatigues, and a yarmulke ripped
from an American flag. "You don't look Jewish," David cracks.
"Yo," Sly replies, wrenching open the chopper's wide green door.
"Hook 'em up, ladies, we're goin' in." It was almost time to jump.

David and I gulp. We don't want to let on this is our first jump.
We avoided all this at Special Forces camp. I tell Rimbaud
we'd love to read his poems, as he shoves Dave out the door.
He grabs my arm. "Anyone ever said you look like Sly Stallone?"
He grunts and thrusts me toward the sky. My helmet cracks
against the jamb, then I'm falling, screaming, most untimely ripped....

Years later, relating this in a Greene Street bar, all of us ripped,
David turns to his date, Jorie, who is wearing a pink yet subtle jump-
suit and Helen Vendler socks. He smiles suavely, then cracks
a pint of Scotch he's hidden in his backpack. "Just our Rambo
daze," he demurs. I look up, astonished: who but our Sly Stallone-
clone, limping toward us, followed by the slamming of the door?

We gape at him. "Yo," he says. He's between us and the door,
have I mentioned? "Hey dude," I smile, "you're looking really ripped,
man." Nothing. "And uh, you know, *buffed!*" "Like Sly Stallone?"
he cries, pounding the table with his fist. We watch our drinks jump.
"You left me in a bind down there, man! Coulda used Rimbaud,

man, help get me out!" Dave and I stare at the linoleum cracks
on our table top. Later, in the john, we were all out of cracks.
Carolyn said her ankles hurt. We carried her out the door,
flagged down a cab. At the Strand, Jorie bought a Rimbaud
comic book some guy in Iowa City drew. I slipped and ripped
my pants. We stopped to watch a cop car give a cab a jump.
On Mulberry Street, the dudes all looked like Sly Stallone.

So we took the girls home, then headed back. No Sly Stallone-
bit tonight. David groans, "We failed him, man." His voice cracks
open: "Should've critiqued his poems, man!" I curse and jump
out of harm's way, as a cab roars by. Dave shoulders the door
into the bar. The Mets are on TV: Scioscia's just ripped
a double down the line. I say again, "It's not our fault, Rambo."

Oh, we made some cracks about Rimbaud and Sly Stallone,
hoisted a few. But guilt's a door, a poem through which you jump
and float, nursing the new asshole you've just been ripped.

David Lehman and Jim Cummins
Parachute Into Iowa City

David Lehman & Jim Cummins Parachute into Iowa City

I got the call at 4 A.M. David said that he'd been up
since three. "It's bad, man," he told me on the phone.
"Just talked to the Head Guy. They've botched surrealism,
man. I know, I know—hard to believe. But it's the real
deal: they take the personal and add blue feathers, man."
Right then I felt a whistling near my heart. "No way,"

I said, thinking of my years there. "No fucking way!"
But it was way. The Head Guy even called Dave up
at home—a breach they usually resisted, to a man—
but time was of the essence here; hence, the phone.
"Chopper's off from Langley now. Let's do the real!"
I grabbed Breton, Eluard, *The Poetry of Surrealism,*

some Reverdy. But how could you botch surrealism?
I wondered. That damn plain song! Was that the way?
But who would buy the trope *you* understood the real?
Who could you fob *that* off on, without cracking up?
No, the students were too smart. But hold the phone—
the LANGUAGE humps—of *course!* "Hey, man!"—

I had to shout above the chopper noise—"Hey, man!
It's *Watten,* man!" We'd dealt with this "surrealism"
before—you mix some kind of bullshit private phone-
mics in the juxtaposition blender—oh, sure, it's a way
to get words on the page. But they just don't hold up.
David grinned, "Down quiet it's too there quiet real—"

109

But then the chaos we jumped into made us reel.
The Maoists from the River Room took out a man
who wrote in forms; the workshops were boarded up.
"They think 'solipsism' is the same as 'surrealism,' "
Dave roared above the roar. "We've *got* to find a way!"
A fiction writing teacher fell; I grabbed her megaphone:

"Let a cat walk through your poem! A homophone
or two! Try juxtaposing Johnny Carson with the real!"
Dave yelled, "Let's try the All-Night Poem! *The Way
is not the way!*" I took it up: "The Way is not the way, man!"
Some heard. A fire chief shouted, "No surrealism
but in things!" It was a start. I gestured, "Keep it up,

man, *yes!*" A mime cried out, "The Way is not the way!
A surface will seduce its depths, and hook the real—
phone sex, a mint, Ben Franklin's ear—*that's* surrealism!"

David Lehman and Jim Cummins
Rescue Denise Duhamel from a
Summer Writers' Conference

David Lehman & Jim Cummins Rescue
Denise Duhamel from a Summer Writers' Conference

"It's not *about* writing—it's a *food chain!*"
I scooped some eggs. The coffee tasted good.
"We've got to rescue her—the numinous
looms like a threat at places like Smarmee!
Though I must say, this coffee is fantastic."
I shrugged, "Last year she said Meat Loaf was great."

Dave groaned. "Of *course* she said Meat Loaf was great—
they let her eat her way up the food chain!
But Smarmee is High Church: you're only good
if you pretend your poems are *numinous!*"
The waitress checked us out. She looked fantastic,
if underwhelmed. "You guys here for Smarmee?"

We feigned indifference. David said, "Smarmee?"
"Don't bullshit me," she laughed. "I think it's great—
Bob Hass's reading last week was fan*tas*tic!"
Her uniform logo read *Le Food Chain.*
"He brought me closer to the…numinous."
I coughed. Dave said, "This coffee's really good!"

"Oh yeah, you're good," I shouted. "Really good!"
Over the hill we could make out Smarmee.
"A glow suffuseth it—it's numinous—"
Dave yelled. I laughed; the chopper's roar felt great.
We hooked up, then descended the food chain.
When we hit, all we heard was "fan*tas*tic!"—

112

seems everybody there was "fan*tas*tic!"
(Except the waiters, who were merely "good.")
A band that called itself the Food Chain
Gang—ephebes granted attendance at Smarmee,
provided they would entertain the great—
hawked that night's gig: Alfred E. Numinous

was reading poems. Dave grinned, "Sound numinous
or ominous to you?" "Oh, just fan*tas*tic!"
Denise sat in the front, eyes glazed, the great
ones heaped about. "Fresh air!" we yelled, got good
grips, lifted her. Then heard the song—"*Smar*-mee!
How we luv ya!"—rocking up the food chain....

The chopper climbed as we three left for good
the numinous food chain they call Smarmee—
where none are really great, but all "fan*tas*tic!"

David Lehman and Jim Cummins
Do Their Part After the World
Trade Center Disaster

David Lehman & Jim Cummins
Do Their Part after the World Trade Center Disaster

Dave and I volunteered for Afghanistan.
The Marine sergeant said we were too old.
"But we want to kill Osama Bin Laden!"
The tough old bird cracked, "So get in line."
Our Langley chief listened, then smiled at us:
"In shooting wars, poets get no respect."

Dave kicked a can as we walked back. "Respect!"
he fumed. "Do they 'respect' Afghanistan?
The symbolism of Cruise missiles got us
into this. It's going to take tropes old
and new to get us out." Waiting on line
to see a film about Osama Bin Laden,

a guy who looked like Osama Bin Laden
was dragged down an alley. "R-E-S-P-E-C-T"
blared out above a record store. The headline
on a newspaper from Afghanistan
urged a jihad. Dave mused, "Maybe some old
anthrax dropped from crop dusters on us?"

As we jaywalked, a taxi nearly hit us.
"Don't worry," I said, "Osama Bin Laden
won't be how *we'll* die." On Duane, an old
man doffed his cap in mocking disrespect,
then begged for change. "I'm From Afghanistan—
Eat Me" his placard read. "Hey, here's a line,"

I said. "'Will Blow Up Domestic Airline
For Food'—what do you think?" "God help us,"
Dave grinned. "*Any* god. Is that Afghanistan
humor? 'Now take Osama Bin Laden—
please!'" "Hey, you assholes show some *respect!*"
I whirled, deflected the blow, used an old

kung fu move to disarm some putz in an old
fireman's hat. His buddy shouted, "I'll line
a birdcage with your face!" "Oh, *that's* respect,"
Dave said, macing him. "You queers hate the U.S.!"
I picked up their flag. "Osama Bin Laden
is hetero," Dave called. "And in Afghanistan."

Downtown, dust covered us. Dave said, "That old
'respect' line's as puerile as Osama Bin Laden."
Dust rose. We dug down, toward Afghanistan.

David Lehman and Jim Cummins
Are Put On Administrative
    Leave

David Lehman & Jim Cummins Are Put on Administrative Leave

Then Langley finally put us out to pasture—
on NPR, a show called *Poet Talk*.
We told our listeners how to fix their art.
As gigs go, this one wasn't all that bad—
line breaks, some tonal problems, nothing big.
Except when someone would bring up "meaning."

Dave would take the point. "You mean *your* meaning
or *my* meaning?" he'd ask. "You mean *Green Pastures*
or *Green Acres*? Or *Green Lantern*? The big
or little meaning, pal? We talk the talk,
but can we walk the walk? Is 'meaning' bad?
Or does our 'meaning' paralyze our art?"

We'd pause, grown quiet at the name of art....
Then I'd make a crack—"We like demeaning
freaks like you!"—and the freak would laugh. "We *bad!*"
Dave would pipe in. "We run this tough love past your
pie hole"—what the heck, the show was *Poet Talk*—
"because the con you represent is big:

your ego, not your meaning, is what's big!"
Not pleasant, but Americans think art
is turning their "profound thoughts" into talk:
"I saw a painting and its deeper meaning
I'll now reveal to you"—as if it passed your
ken, not your inspection. "But that's so bad!"

they'd cry. "You're so unkind! Even the bad
art must be coddled, reassured it's big!"
"Who reassures us of greener pastures?"
David offers. "God's dead. So is most art."
That starts the howls. "We *need* to find meaning
in life and art! That's not just pillow talk!"

By then the theme music to *Poet Talk*
is drowning out all comments, good or bad.
That's what themes do: repeat the dull meanings
until they're thought profound, inspired, big.
"Next week," I yell, "we'll look at how the art
of line breaks leads us to...greener pastures."

"*Greener pastures*'!" I guffaw. "Woo, big talk!"
"*Pie hole*'?" Dave hoots. "Now *there's* 'profound meaning'!"
We slap five. "Good radio, bad art!"

Jim Cummins and David Lehman
Defeat the Masked Man

Jim Cummins & David Lehman Defeat the Masked Man

Finally, he spoke. "Which one of you is David?"
Jim looked at me and I looked at Jim, like a pair
of outfielders who let an easy fly ball drop
between them. Finally, I spoke: "Give me the gun."
"Give him the gun," Jim said, trying to sound
as calm as Brueghel's ship that had somewhere

to get to, as we did not. A ball falls somewhere
and Jim goes in one direction, while in the other David
scurries, as the tying run scores, the sound
of exultant cheering fills the stadium, and the hapless pair
are traded to the American League. "Give him the gun,"
Jim repeated. The man's hands were shaking. "Drop

it." And he did. Poetry had rendered the gun harmless as a drop
of rain on the outfield grass in a dream sestina. Somewhere
a bell rings, and a little boy playing with his father's gun
goes off looking for the nearest Goliath, emulating David.
The masked man conceded the pot to Jim, holder of a pair
of aces. Finally, he spoke: "What's that sound?"

"I didn't hear anything," Jim said. "What sound?"
In the fog you couldn't see the moon drop
like a ball of light. We cuffed the masked man. A pair
of jacks trumps deuces but loses to a flush, and somewhere
a betting man gets ready to put in all his chips. David
clapped Jim on the back. "I knew you'd get the gun."

Finally, he spoke: "We're Yanks. Every man his own gun.
We have reviewed our financial portfolios and they're sound.
We have hired Jim to be bartender and David
to be bouncer at the sestina bar, where you can drop
a hundred bucks on a hand or a line. Welcome to somewhere
else I have never traveled." The people cheered. What a pair

of jokers, one girl said, and everyone laughed. The appear-
ance of David and Jim at this climactic moment, guns
in hand, struck many as too good to be true. Somewhere
they had never traveled past lighthouses on Long Island Sound
where in a chilled glass of gin you can taste the single drop
of vermouth, and Jim writes sestinas about his exploits with David.

David turned to Jim. "What have you got?" "Pair
of queens." "How did we get that guy to drop the gun?"
Somewhere you could hear a cheer, an echo without sound.

To Jim Cummins and David Lehman
on the Opening of
the Sestina Bar

To Jim Cummins & David Lehman
on the Opening of the Sestina Bar

I'm so glad to hear you've opened the sestina bar.
Have you plans to franchise in Mississippi?
I hope so. One gets so very short
around here on sestinas.
Oh sure, I've got material, a whole bunch of ideas
lined up and backlit like top-shelf bottles,

but sometimes I feel like I have to put on my coke bottles
just to see what goes good together. I need a bar-
tender, see? A bouncer, too, would be a good idea,
maybe. I mean, images come so fast in Mississippi—
you can feel a bit claustrophobic without even attempting a sestina!
But a bouncer, he could help arrange lines, short-

list the ideas, or even make the bad ones less short-
sighted, could steer me through the bottle-
neck of the coda, the hardest part of any sestina,
bar
none. We've got a lot of invasive kudzu in Mississippi
and the whole "landscape is psychology" idea

is what gives me the idea
that we're a little short
on the restraint demanded by the form (ironic, since "one-Mississippi,
two-Mississippi" is how we measured restraint, counting aloud as kids, bottled
up with excitement, when playing kick-the-can or monkey bars
or capture-the-flag). So how am I supposed to write a sestina

without your help when the sestina's
main idea
is to be rigid as a bar
code and I'm living in this mixed up state and Irish to boot—a redhead and short
fused as a bottle
rocket, which, incidentally, is legal in Mississippi?

Think about the fireworks all over Mississippi
at the grand opening of your saloon. We could play Tina
Turner! It's practically a license to bottle
money. Which depresses me a bit—sometimes I feel all the good ideas
were taken right before I thought of them, and I'm short-
changed as usual. But still, a joint like yours could raise the bar

in Mississippi. Sirs, please let me know soon. I'm getting tired of bar-
gaining. It's got a short shelf life, rather like a sestina,
this idea. Someone could beat us to it, sail away like a ship in a bottle.

Echo

Echo

Lovers check each other—"How are you?"—
when love is going, but before it's gone.
"Oh, I'm better. The nausea's settled down.
The mad howling stopped the other night."
Some rueful laughter on the other end.
"Me, too," she whispers, in her quiet voice,

"me, too." He thinks: I love her quiet voice.
"Yesterday, at the market, I saw you—"
she catches, laughs. It's hard for love to end.
It's hard to wake up, certain that it's gone.
He says, "I thought about you all last night,
but I'm better. The nausea's settled down."

They never say that love has settled down,
that it no longer uses its sweet voice
to carry them in boats across the night.
If you deny love, love will deny you;
the nighttime of its daytime voice is gone,
as you will be. It's hard for love to end.

But any love is difficult to end—
all endings seem to whisper, then lie down,
an old man dying by the fire, soon gone,
as if he'd never lived. Her quiet voice,
that only yesterday spoke just to you,
will soon become a whisper in the night,

then disappear forever from the night.
And there's no preparation for that end.
She laughs again. "I want to be with you."
He understands. He puts the phone back down.
How will he live without her quiet voice?
What will he do, when she's finally gone?

Within a week the moving van is gone.
He works all day, and dreads the quiet night.
The day will come when he'll forget her voice;
he has no need or longing for that end.
He'd settle now for keeping dinner down.
He hears again: "*I want to be with you.*"

He stares into the pool of night, her voice
behind him, gone. He monitors the end:
he lies down, hears the faint refrain: "...*with you*..."

The Old Constellation

The Old Constellation

The old constellation of wish, word, guilt, pleasure, shame. —Judith Hall

Other people go to bed. I just sit and wish
for nothing much, just to know the word
when I hear it and not to feel the guilt
that other people associate with pleasure,
or something more primal than guilt, shame,
which is what you get for having a body.

What can be worse than not having a body?
(In my veins there is a wish.)
Money is to shit as guilt is to shame
as the sentence is to the word.
Is that understood? It's been a pleasure
to serve you, said the Commissioner of Guilt.

Some soldiers can kill without feeling guilt.
I learned I wasn't one of them. I was anybody
in a uniform, and staying alive wasn't a pleasure
but a duty. Some of the injured wished
they had died, a wish seldom put into words
without feelings of shame.

If the women we loved were unashamed,
it was because they obeyed the laws of guilt
and loved the men who wooed them with words
in praise of their yielding bodies.
I asked her, did she get her wish?
She said yes but it gave her no pleasure.

The poem's first purpose is to give pleasure
and defeat the formidable forces of shame
that would twist every healthy lusty wish
into a dark confession of guilt
and a renunciation of the body:
the word without flesh, the naked, shivering word.

I who believe in the constellations of the word
would construct a planetarium of pleasure
for my friends, where each heavenly body
can be contemplated without the shame
of a pretty librarian or the guilt
of a veteran who pulled the trigger of a wish.

The word is the result of the wish for the word.
Not every pleasure is a guilty one.
A shame it would be to forsake love's body.

The Hotel Fiesta Sestina

The Hotel Fiesta Sestina

As fingerprints to a detective are a painter's brushstrokes
to critics who reveal themselves by their choice of hotel
in foreign cities where the weather is inner
and an impassive tuxedo-clad angel may dance the tango
with a nude in bright hues, and later they get to eat breakfast
in bed and talk about modern art and its wonders.

We needed great paintings in a world without wonders.
But then concepts replaced paintings. It was a masterstroke
some guy in marketing wrote on a napkin at breakfast
where the coffee was weak at the conventioneers' hotel.
Our parents learned dances like the tango.
And what do we do? Nothing. We go inner.

I took a journey into the interior, where your inner
child met the adult I was when I was a boy. Of all wonders
I have known, this still seems to me supreme, this tango
of male and female, stroke and counterstroke,
her dress on a hanger in the closet of the hotel,
near the ocean, nothing fancy, a little bed and breakfast.

The meal of the day the couple craves is breakfast.
He reads the newspaper while her thoughts turn inner.
She does the math. Do two by night in a grand hotel
equal three by day on a beach? Yes, and no wonder
we display the dildo of our truest self at the stroke
of midnight when we commence upon our last tango.

133

Every time we dance is the last time we dance the tango.
In the morning, gazes averted, we eat a guilty breakfast.
We stutter like elderly victims of a stroke.
Part of me is still inside you; yet your inner
self's now closed to me, not close to me, and I wonder
if we will ever again consummate our longing in this hotel

where adulterers pretend to be businessmen and hotel
owners' wives turn out to be spies. I loved the tango
of early morning, a big bathtub, a slow breakfast,
and still do, because of you. The wonder
is not that our bodies resist the menacing stroke
of hours but that each poor lover's a sinner.

In an inner chamber at our first hotel
where the tango was a stroke of genius,
you were wonderful, and then we had breakfast.

Contents

Acknowledgments

Poems from this book have appeared in the following periodicals and anthologies, which we gratefully acknowledge:

American Poetry Review, the *Antioch Review, Boulevard, Chariton Review,* the *Cincinnati Review, Euphony, Flights,* the *Journal, LIT,* the *Los Angeles Review, McSweeney's, Open City,* the *Paris Review, Shenandoah,* the *Times Literary Supplement, Tin House,* and four volumes of *The Best American Poetry* series: 1988, 1994, 1995, and 1998.

"The 39 Steps" was first published in *An Alternative to Speech* by David Lehman (Princeton University Press, 1986). Copyright © 1986 by David Lehman; reprinted by permission. "Operation Memory" was first published in *Operation Memory* by David Lehman (Princeton University Press, 1990). Copyright © 1990 by David Lehman; reprinted by permission. "Sestina (for Jim Cummins)," "Big Hair," "Sestina: When he called the lawyer," "The Prophet's Lantern," "End Note," "Jim Cummins & David Lehman Defeat the Masked Man," and "The Old Constellation" were first published in *When a Woman Loves a Man* by David Lehman (Scribner, 2005). Copyright © 2005 by David Lehman; reprinted by permission.

"Fling," "The Body Is the Flower," and "Romantic Love" were first published in *Portrait in a Spoon* by James Cummins (University of South Carolina Press, 1997). Copyright © 1997 by James Cummins; reprinted by permission. "The World's Trade," "Echo," and "Collegiality" were first published in *Then & Now* by James Cummins (The Swallow Press/Ohio University Press, 2004). Copyright © 2004 by James Cummins; reprinted by permission.

About the Collaborators

James Cummins is the author of *The Whole Truth,* a collection of sestinas about the television lawyer Perry Mason, *Then and Now,* and *Portrait in a Spoon.* He was born in Columbus, Ohio, and grew up in Cleveland and Indianapolis. He received his MFA from the University of Iowa and is curator of the Elliston Poetry Collection at the University of Cincinnati, where he also teaches.

David Lehman is on the core faculty of the graduate writing program at the New School. In 1988 he launched *The Best American Poetry* series. He is the author of six poetry collections, most recently *When a Woman Loves a Man* (Scribner, 2005). He lives in New York City and Ithaca, New York.

Archie Rand has had more than one hundred solo exhibitions, and his work is displayed in major museums worldwide, including the Metropolitan Museum of Art, the San Francisco Museum of Modern Art, the Chicago Art Institute, the Victoria and Albert Museum (London), the Bibliothèque Nationale of Paris, and the Tel Aviv Museum of Art. He is currently the Presidential Professor of Art at Brooklyn College and is the former chair of the Visual Art Department at Columbia University. Rand has previously collaborated on many illustrated poetry projects with Robert Creeley, John Ashbery, John Yau, Clark Coolidge, and many others.